Toilet Paper Origami
on a Roll

DECORATIVE FOLDS AND FLOURISHES
FOR OVER-THE-TOP HOSPITALITY

LINDA WRIGHT

To the lights of my life, Randy and John

Toilet Paper Origami on a Roll:
Decorative Folds and Flourishes for Over-the-Top Hospitality

www.tporigami.com

Other books by Linda Wright

Toilet Paper Origami:
Delight your Guests with Fancy Folds and Simple Surface Embellishments

and

Toilet Paper Crafts for Holidays and Special Occasions:
60 Papercraft, Sewing, Origami and Kanzashi Projects

Edition 1.0

Lindaloo Enterprises
P.O. Box 90135
Santa Barbara, CA 93190
sales@lindaloo.com

ISBN: 9780980092332

Library of Congress Control Number: 2012911671

CONTENTS

INTRODUCTION

An artfully folded roll of toilet paper will add joy and memorability to any bathroom—on land or sea, at a home or hotel, on a luxury yacht—or even in a public restroom stall. The success of my first book on the subject, *Toilet Paper Origami*, has demonstrated that people far and wide are having fun with this whimsical touch of hospitality.

Toilet Paper Origami on a Roll came about because of one particular design—the Bodacious Bow. There's nothing better than a beautiful bow—and I was elated to develop a way to easily make one without tying. It was love at first fold...and meant to be shared. Fresh inspiration followed, and this new collection was conceived. *Toilet Paper Origami on a Roll* contains many new designs for standard horizontal toilet paper holders—including folds for holidays and special occasions plus popular hospitality motifs. It also provides styles for vertical holders, styles for those who like their toilet paper to hang under the roll, and styles for spare rolls thoughtfully displayed within reach.

These projects were designed to be fun, fast and easy. The step-by-step photographs will lead you along the way; just keep your eye on the next picture as you are folding. Toilet papers differ widely in texture, weight, and decorative embossing patterns. Some excel for creasing, others for draping. I suggest experimenting with the brands in your area. Some origami designs, such as the Topknot or Pretty Posy, work nicely with a soft paper; others, such as the Shooting Star, with crisp. For some styles, such as the Lovely Heart, I prefer thin paper; for others, such as Upsy Daisy, I prefer thick. And sometimes I choose a particular paper just for its embossing. An appropriately embossed design will complement and enhance your work—such as a pattern of fanciful dots and swirls for the Celebration Cake. Toilet paper products tend to change frequently, and just as you develop a favorite, it may be modified. Luckily, there are always plenty of options. To learn more about my choices for the projects in this book, visit my website at www.tporigami.com.

Now for some final starting tips:
- Throughout this book, a "square" refers to one sheet of toilet paper between perforations. Squares should measure approximately 4x4 inches, but they are rarely perfectly square. Toilet paper origami is very forgiving and this won't affect your result. Once in awhile I come across a brand that is perforated as half-sized sheets. In this case, adjust your work accordingly.
- Fanfolding or pleating refers to a zigzag fold in which parallel folds of equal width are made in the manner of an accordion.
- When spare toilet paper rolls are displayed, they can be placed either horizontally or vertically in vessels of metal, glass, wood, bamboo or basketry. Try oblong trays, shallow bowls, pillar candle holders, or even a pedestal plate.
- Add a floral or fruity fragrance to toilet paper rolls by placing several drops of essential oil inside the cardboard core. Essential oils are fragrances extracted from leaves, flowers, stems, roots or bark—such as rose, jasmine, geranium, lavender, orange or lemon. The scent will waft pleasantly each time the paper is pulled.

Toilet Paper Origami on a Roll is all about over-the-top hospitality. Use it to brand a business, make a hotel memorable, or surprise your friends and family. It's a perfect potty-training reward for toddlers, and a delight for anyone. Best of all, toilet paper origami will make someone smile. I invite you to discover this fun-filled craft. Let's roll!

simple elegance

Understated yet classy, this starter style can be folded in seconds.

1 Unwind a short length of toilet paper from the roll. Fold right corner up to left edge.

2 Rewind the roll.

3 Finished.

frill

This pleat-and-twist favorite is easy as can be—and such a delicate delight.

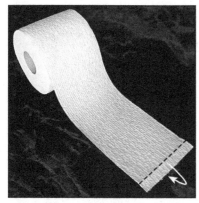

1 Unwind several squares. Fold raw edge under ½ inch.

2 Fanfold until you have pleated 2 squares.

3 Stack pleats on top of paper flowing from the roll.

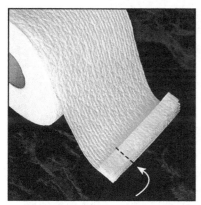

4 About 1 inch from edge—twist left side of stack upward. Pinch the twist tightly to keep it in place.

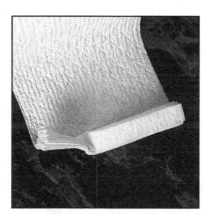

5 Rewind the roll. Place your thumb on the twist, and pull gently downward on the lowest pleat to fan out the folds.

6 Finished.

tulip

This enchanting tulip is almost too pretty to pick!

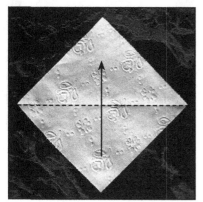

1   Tulip: Tear off 1 square. Fold in half diagonally.

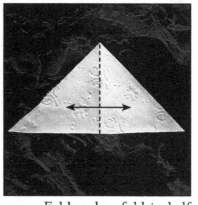

2   Fold and unfold in half to make a crease.

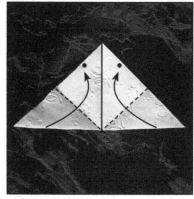

3   Fold the lower edges up to the dots.

4   Fold right and left sides to the back.

5   Set tulip aside.

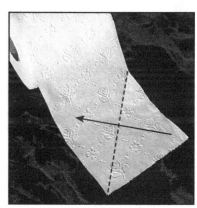

6   Vessel: Fold right corner up to left side.

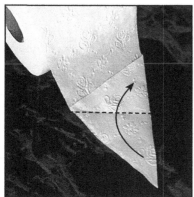

7   Fold tip to right corner.

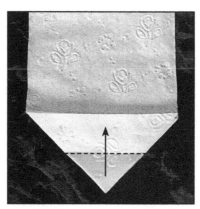

8   Fold tip to raw edge.

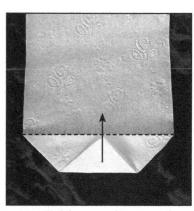

9   Fold up at the raw edge.

10 Fold corners to the center back.

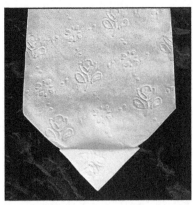

11 Rewind the roll.

12 Insert tulip.

13 Finished.

Tip: Give your tulip some scent with several drops of floral essential oil inside the cardboard core.

bodacious bow

Rip, wrap, and roll to make this beautiful bow—no tying required.
Optional supply: cardboard

1 Tear off a 2-square strip of toilet paper and a 4-square strip. Set them aside.

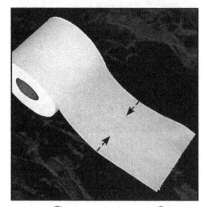

2 Center piece: Locate the first perforation. Tear each side along the perforation leaving a 1-inch section intact at the center. See Step 3 for a helpful tip.

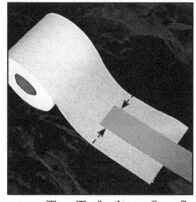

3 Tip: To facilitate Step 2, cut a 1 x 6-inch piece of cardboard. Place cardboard as shown. Press down on cardboard and tear up to each edge.

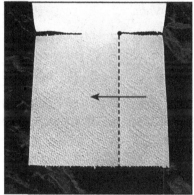

4 Fold right side inward at the dot.

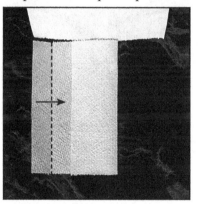

5 Fold left side inward so that raw edges meet.

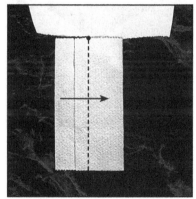

6 Fold left side inward at the dot.

7 Set the toilet paper roll aside. Get the 4-square strip from Step 1.

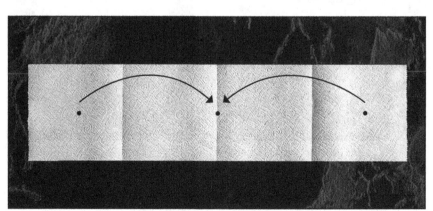

8 Loop: Fold ends inward so that middle of right and left squares meets the center perforation. *Do not crease.*

15

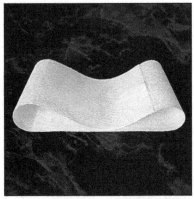

9   Tail: Place the 2-square strip from Step 1 on top of the loop.

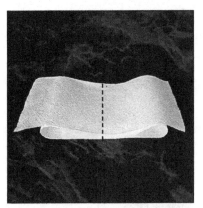

10   Pinch and pleat paper across the center until the edges meet.

11   Place your work, loop-side down, at middle of center piece.

12   Fold lower dot to upper dot.

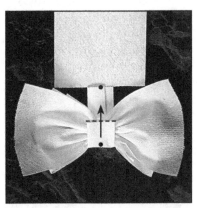

13   Fold lower dot to upper dot, flipping the bow over as you fold.

14   Press firmly on center to set bow in place. Rewind the roll.

15   Pull tail ends downward—using care not to tear the perforations that connect the bow to the roll.

16   Press on the center to secure bow to roll. Finished.

Tip: Try making the tail of your bow longer for a different look. Cut the tail ends at an angle, if desired. The bow on the cover of this book was made using a 3-square tail with ends cut at angles.

16

swimming swan

1 Upper Swan: Tear off 1 square. Fold and unfold in half diagonally to make a crease.

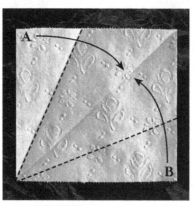

2 Fold Points A and B to the center crease.

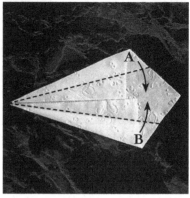

3 Fold Points A and B to the center.

4 Fold in half lengthwise.

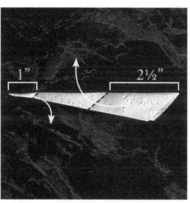

5 Fold the right side up. Fold the left tip down.

6 Set swan aside.

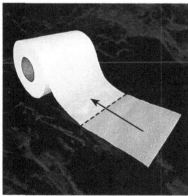

7 Lower Swan: Fold the first square up—using the perforation as your foldline.

8 Fold raw edge down at an angle, tapering the fold as shown.

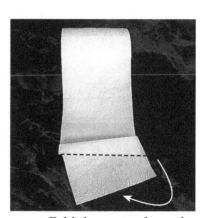

9 Fold lower end to the back matching your foldline to the edge of the bottom layer.

10 Fold right and left sides under, adjusting the folds to make a centered vessel.

11 Rewind the roll by grasping end between your index and middle fingers while applying gentle tension with your other hand.

12 Place Upper Swan into the vessel. Align the swan's neck with the left edge of the pocket.

13 Finished.

Tip: Use a ballpoint pen to draw an eye on the swan, if desired.

grand teton

This snow-capped peak commemorates my favorite mountain in Jackson Hole, Wyoming.

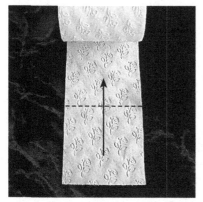

1 With toilet paper flowing *under* the roll, fold the first square up. The perforations will be your fold-line.

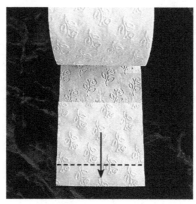

2 Fold the raw edge down in a 1-inch fold.

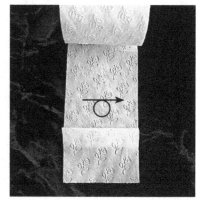

3 Flip horizontally so that the toilet paper is flowing *over* the roll.

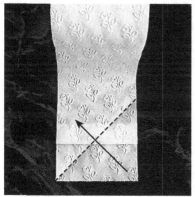

4 Fold the right corner up to the left side.

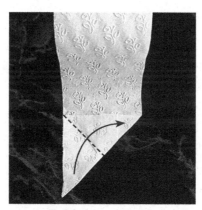

5 Fold the tip to the right corner.

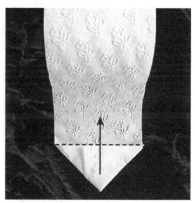

6 Fold the triangle up.

7 Rewind roll so that the mountain rests across the center.

8 Finished.

lovely heart

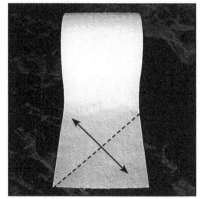

1   Fold and unfold right corner to left side to make a crease.

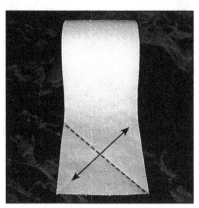

2   Fold and unfold left corner to right side to make a crease.

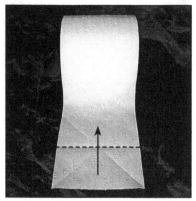

3   You will see a creased "X". Fold lower edge up at the center of the "X".

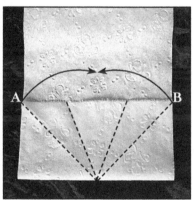

4   Fold corners A and B of the top layer up to the center.

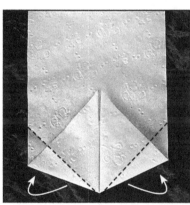

5   Fold lower edges to the back.

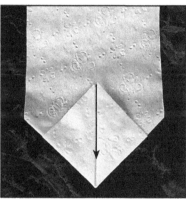

6   Pull top of diamond forward to flip diamond over.

7   Fold tips to the dots. Crease firmly.

8   Fold tips to the dots. Crease firmly.

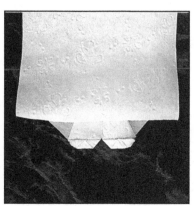

9   Flip your work to the front.

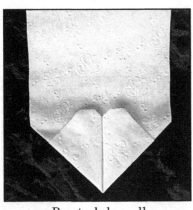

10 Rewind the roll.

11 Finished.

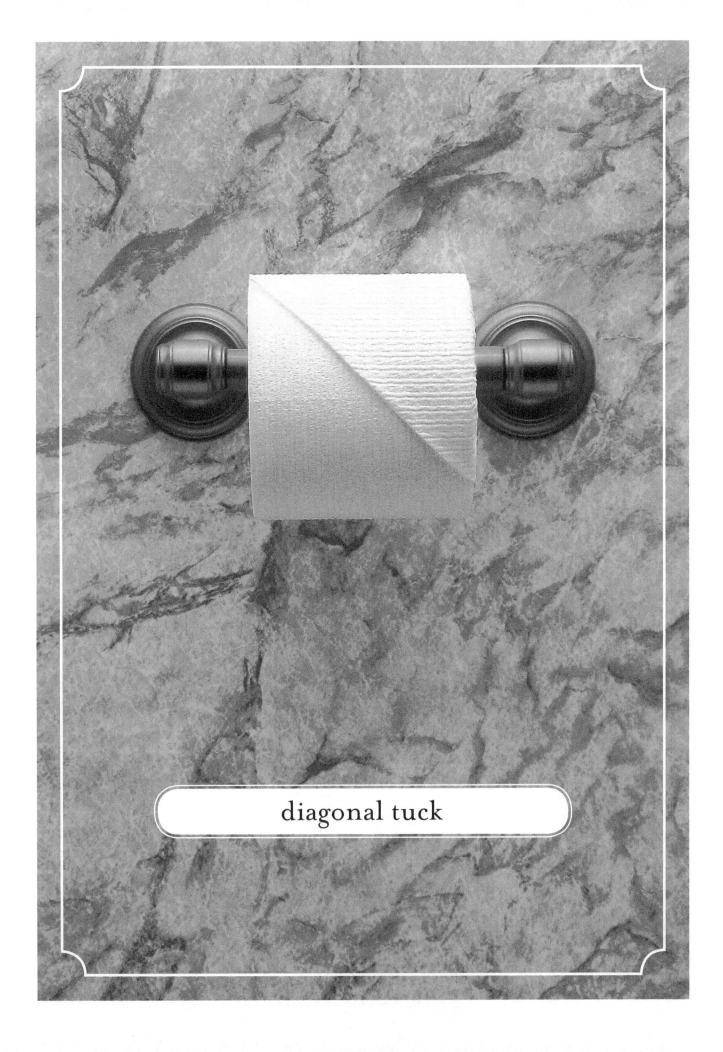

diagonal tuck

The diagonal tuck can be used as a neat and tidy finish on its own—for any orientation of toilet paper holder. It is also used as the foundation for several upcoming designs.

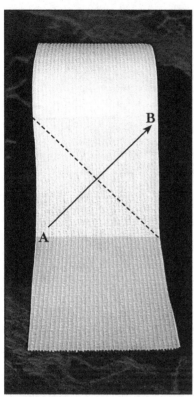

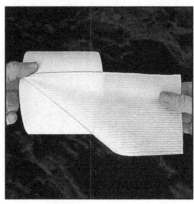

1   Fold Point A up to Point B. (Point A is on the 1st perforation and Point B is on the 2nd perforation.)

2   Crease the fold. Tuck the excess paper into the core.

3   Finished.

plume

Display a spare roll with panache—or use this style with a vertical toilet paper holder.

1 Tear off six 2-square strips of toilet paper and stack them going in different directions.

2 Prepare the roll with a diagonal tuck (see page 29). Place the stack of strips on top of the roll.

3 Gently push the paper down into the core with a fingertip...

4 ...like this. Adjust the folds into a pretty shape.

5 Finished.

Tip: Vary the number of strips used in Step 1 for different degrees of fullness.

celebration cake

Whether the occasion is a birthday, wedding, or anniversary, this design takes the cake!
Choose toilet paper with a fancy embossing pattern to enhance your presentation.

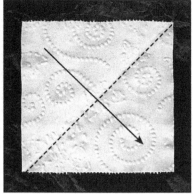

1 Flame: Tear off 1 square. Fold in half diagonally.

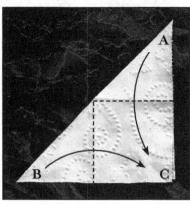

2 Fold Points A and B to Point C.

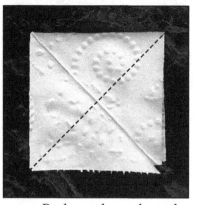

3 Push and pucker the paper along the dotted line with your fingertips until the end points meet. Twist the lower half tightly.

4 Press your thumb into the untwisted end to mold it into a nice flame shape. Set flame aside.

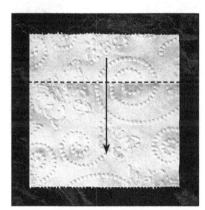

5 Candlestick: Tear off 1 square. Fold upper edge down about 1¼ inches.

6 Place twisted end of flame at Point A.

7 Roll rectangle around twisted end of flame.

8 Seam is center back of candle. Spin flame to face the candle front. Set candle aside.

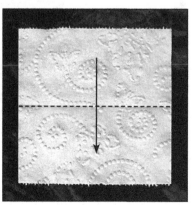

9 Upper Tier: Tear off 1 square. Fold in half.

33

10 Place candle at center, right side down.

11 Fold the left and right sides to the center.

12 Set upper tier aside.

13 Lower Tier: Unwind a short length of paper from the roll. Fold the first square under.

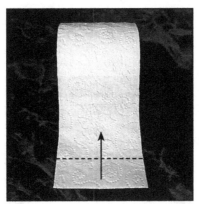

14 Fold the end up about 1½ inches.

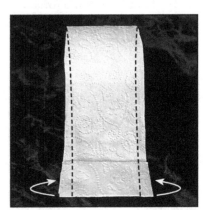

15 Fold the corners under ¾ inch, adjusting folds to make a centered tier for your cake.

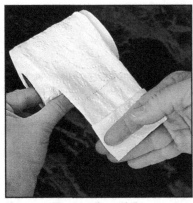

16 Rewind roll by grasping the end between your index and middle fingers while applying gentle tension with your other hand.

17 Insert upper tier into lower tier.

18 Finished.

Tip: The center back seam of the candlestick can be glued in place with hand lotion, if desired. Squirt a small amount of lotion, about the size of a pea, into the palm of your hand. Use a fingertip to spread a thin layer under the seam. Press lightly. Let it dry.

cornucopia

The cornucopia is a symbol of abundant supply.

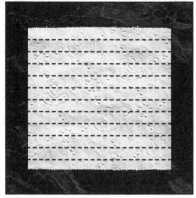

1 Fan: Tear of 1 square. Fanfold in tiny pleats.

2 Compress the pleats into a stack.

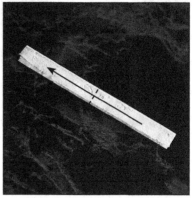

3 Fold in half, pinching the crease tightly.

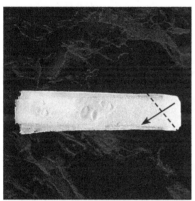

4 Fold tip down; pinch the crease tightly.

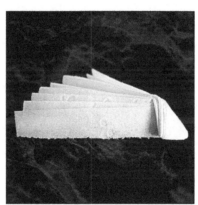

5 Set fan aside.

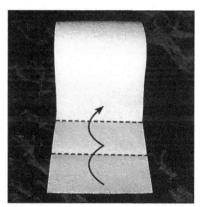

6 Vessel: With TP flowing *over* the roll, unwind a short length of paper. Fold the end up twice, making each fold about 1¾ inches deep.

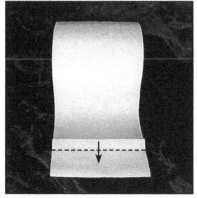

7 Fold the top edge down ½ inch.

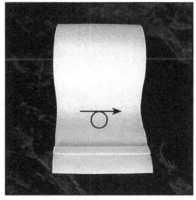

8 Flip your work so that the toilet paper is flowing *under* the roll.

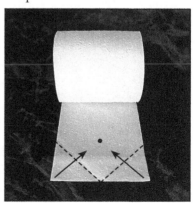

9 Fold corners up to the center.

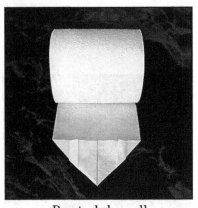

10 Rewind the roll.

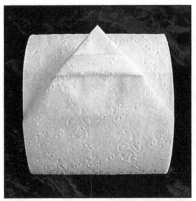

11 Place fan in vessel, tapered side up.

12 Finished.

diamond crest

1 Crest: Tear off 1 square. Fold in half diagonally.

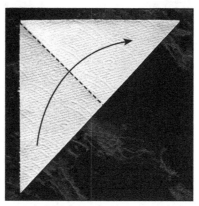

2 Fold lower tip up to the right tip.

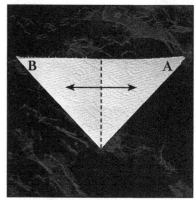

3 Fold and unfold Point A to Point B, top layer only, to make a crease.

4 Insert index finger into top right layer. Raise right half of triangle to vertical.

5 Position diamond shape at center of triangle. Flatten into place.

6 Set the crest aside.

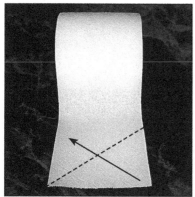

7 Diamond: Unwind several squares from the roll. Fold right corner up to left side.

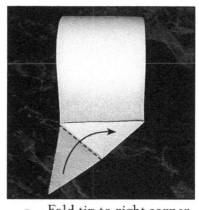

8 Fold tip to right corner.

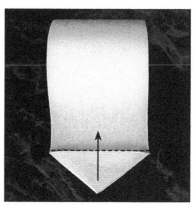

9 Fold triangle up.

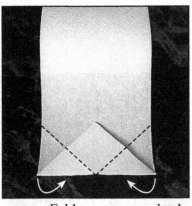

10 Fold corners to back, adjusting angle of folds to make a symmetric diamond.

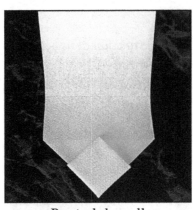

11 Rewind the roll.

12 Insert crest.

13 Finished.

topknot

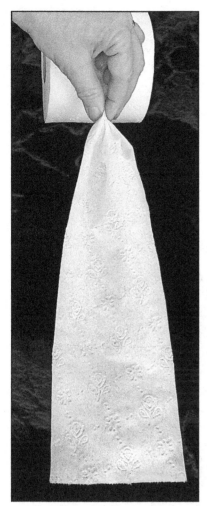

1 Unwind 3 squares and gently pinch paper at the third perforation. Twist the strand loosely.

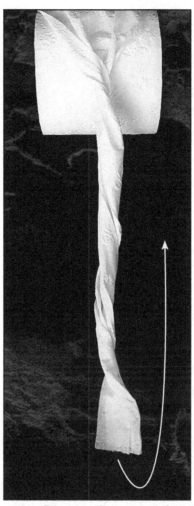

2 Bring tail up to make a "U" shape near the roll.

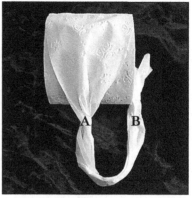

3 Place Point B under Point A to make a 2-inch loop.

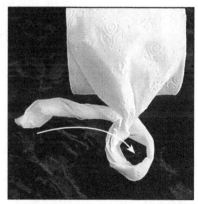

4 Push end down through front of loop.

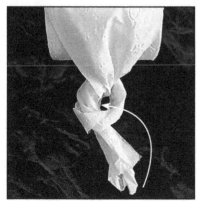

5 Wrap end over rim of loop and tuck it into the center.

6 Rewind roll and adjust knot to sit at the center. Press gently on knot to secure it in place, if necessary.

7 Finished.

palm tree

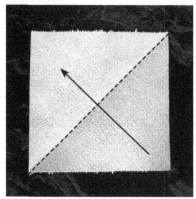

1 Palm Frond: Tear off 1 square. Fold it in half diagonally.

2 Pucker the paper with your fingertips along the dotted line until the ends points meet...

3 ...to look like this. Twist at the center to secure.

4 Repeat to make as many fronds as desired. You can make a Palm Tree with 3, 4 or 5 fronds. Set fronds aside.

5 Unwind a bit of TP from the roll. Tear along the first perforation at each side, leaving a 1½-inch section intact at the center. See Step 6 for a helpful tip.

6 Tip: To make Step 5 easier, cut a piece of cardboard 1½ x 6 inches. Place cardboard as shown. Press down on cardboard and tear up to each edge.

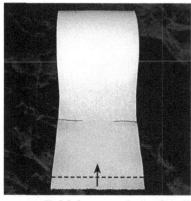

7 Fold lower edge of roll up in a ¾-inch fold.

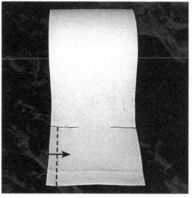

8 Fold the left side inward in a ½-inch fold.

9 Stack the palm fronds with their curved edge up, and arrange them as you would like them to look on your tree. Place fronds against end of toilet paper...

47

10 ...like this. Fold the right side inward, tapering the fold slightly toward the fronds.

11 Fold the left side inward. Be sure to wrap securely around twisted area of fronds.

12 Fold the palm tree up.

13 Rewind roll until palm tree rests in place.

14 Finished.

Tip: To secure your palm tree to the roll, glue it with a little bit of hand lotion, if desired. Squirt a small amount of lotion, about the size of a pea, into the palm of your hand. Use a fingertip to spread a thin layer along the back of the trunk. Press trunk against roll. Let it dry.

fontainebleau

In 2006, as part of a $1 billion renovation, the 5-star Fontainebleau Hotel in Miami Beach, Florida replaced a folded point on the end of their toilet paper rolls with this fold—to give customers an impression that the hotel was special. This simple style is well-suited for the embellishments in the last chapter.

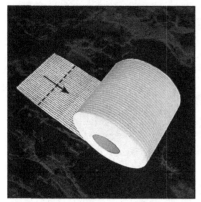

1 Fold the first square in half.

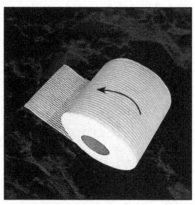

2 Rewind the paper, positioning the crease at the middle of the roll.

3 Finished.

The Fontainebleau Hotel, pronounced "fountain blue", is renowned as the most magnificent hotel on Miami Beach. Built in 1953 as the epitomy of glamour, it became a favorite destination for celebrities. Through the years, numerous television shows, movies, and records have been filmed and recorded at this famous location. In the early days, tourists were charged a fee just to view this grand hotel. Guests at the Fontainebleau can expect a luxury experience from start to finish—with attention to detail in every amenity.

Today, the Fontainebleau Hotel is recognized in the United States as a historic and architectural landmark. In 2008, it was added to the U.S. National Register of Historic Places. In 2012, the Florida Chapter of the American Institute of Architects ranked the Fontainebleau #1 on its list of *Florida Architecture: 100 Years. 100 Places.*

Sources: Fontainebleau Miami Beach, http://en.wikipedia.org/w/index.php?title=Fontainebleau_Miami_Beach&oldid=500098813 (last visited June 22, 2012) and Hotel toilet paper folding, http://en.wikipedia.org/w/index.php?title=Hotel_toilet_paper_folding&oldid=496698799 (last visited June 22, 2012).

pillar candle

Use this design for a spare roll. For the perfect presentation, place it on a 5-inch diameter pillar candle holder.

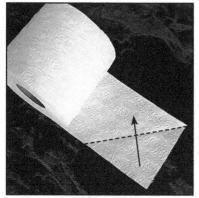

1 Fold left corner up to right edge.

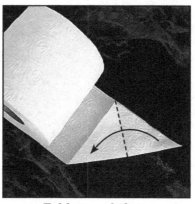

2 Fold tip to left corner.

3 Unwind a short length of paper from the roll.

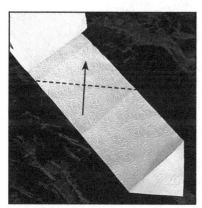

4 Locate the 2nd square from the end; fold in half diagonally across the square.

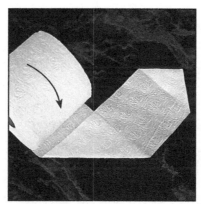

5 Rewind the roll.

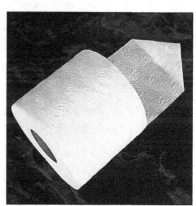

6 Set the roll upright on its core.

7 Tuck the tail, but not the pointed end, into the core.

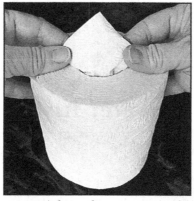

8 Adjust the point to make a pretty flame.

9 Finished.

water lily

1 Lily petal: Tear off 1 square. Fold in half diagonally. (Most TP squares are not perfectly square—so your edges may not line up exactly.)

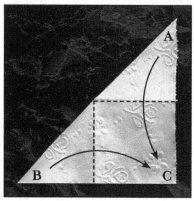

2 Fold Points A and B to Point C.

3 Push and pucker the paper along the dotted line with your fingertips until the end points meet. Twist the lower half tightly.

4 Press your thumb into the untwisted end to mold it into a pretty petal shape. Repeat Steps 1-4 to make 4 more petals.

5 Center piece: Tear off 2 squares. Crumple 1 square into a tight ball and place in center of 2nd square. Wrap square over ball; twist ends together tightly.

6 Place petals around the center piece...

7 ...like this. Wrap tape around twisted ends to secure petals in place.

8 Set flower aside.

9 Vase: Fold raw edge up to the first perforation; then fold the end up again—*on* the perforation. The folds will be approximately 2-inches deep.

55

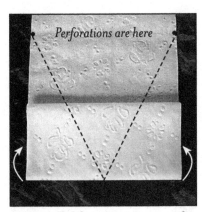

Perforations are here

10 Fold corners to the back: angle the folds from center front to the next row of perforations (see dots).

11 Rewind the roll.

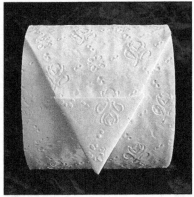

12 Place water lily in vase.

13 Finished.

Tip: Give your flower some fragrance by placing several drops of floral essential oil inside the cardboard core.

fanburst

This style is best suited for recessed toilet paper holders so that the fan can rest against the wall for stability.
Additional supply: hand lotion

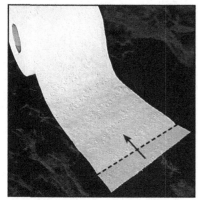

1 Fold the end up about ¾ inch.

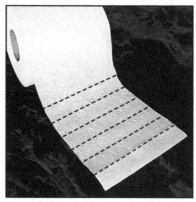

2 Continue to fanfold until you have made 6 more creases—for a total of 7 creases.

3 Stack pleats on top of roll.

4 Spread a thin layer of hand lotion on half of the stack—top layer only—to glue the top folds together. Crease stack at center by folding the sides up.

5 Pinch the crease tightly to strengthen the fold. Gently release pleats.

6 Arrange folds in a pretty fan shape on top of roll. Finished.

pretty posy

Create a fun little flower by coiling a rope of tightly twisted toilet tissue.

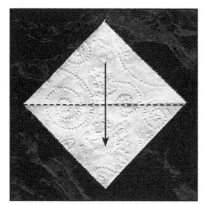

1 Leaves: Tear off 1 square. Fold it in half diagonally.

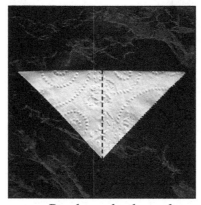

2 Pinch and pleat along the dotted line with your fingertips until the end points meet. Twist twice. Pinch the twist tightly to flatten it out.

3 Set leaves aside.

4 Flower: Unwind some toilet paper from the roll. Pinch paper across the middle of the 4th square. Twist the tail to make a tight rope...

5 ...that looks like this. Now complete Steps 6-7 without letting go of the rope.

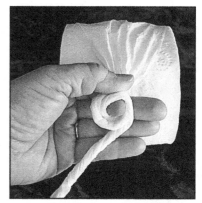

6 Starting at top of twisted rope, wind it around your index finger several times, overlapping each wrap.

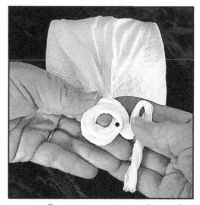

7 Stop wrapping when the rope is at the 3 o'clock position (see dot) and fold the rope. Push the crease up from behind—thru center of flower.

61

8 Position flower at center of roll and press into place. The tail of the rope is the flower stem; twist the end into a point. Place leaves under stem.

9 Finished.

candlestick

There's nothing like a candle to make a bathroom feel cozy!

1 Flame: Tear off 1 square. Fold in half diagonally.

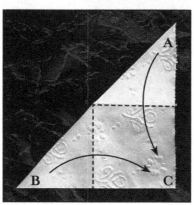

2 Fold Points A and B to Point C.

3 Push and pucker the paper along the dotted line with your fingertips until the end points meet. Twist the lower half tightly.

4 Press your thumb into untwisted end to mold it into a nice flame shape. Set flame aside.

5 Candlestick: Tear off 1 square. Fold in half.

6 Place twisted end of flame at Point A.

7 Roll rectangle around twisted end of flame.

8 Seam is center back of candle. Spin flame to face candle front. Set candle aside.

9 Handle: Tear 1 square off of the roll. Fold in half diagonally.

10 Starting at Point A, roll it up...

11 ...like this...to make a narrow tube. Then twist the paper tightly, leaving about 1 inch untwisted at each end.

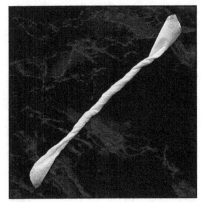

12 Bring ends together to make a loop; then twist the ends to each other to secure the loop.

13 Set handle aside.

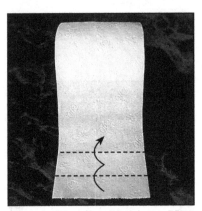

14 Candle Holder: Unwind a short length of paper from the roll. Fold the end up twice in 1-inch folds.

15 Fold right and left corners to the underside.

16 Rewind the roll.

17 Insert handle at right side and candle at center.

18 Finished.

Tip: The center back seam of the candlestick can be glued in place with hand lotion, if desired. Squirt a small amount of lotion, about the size of a pea, into the palm of your hand. Use a fingertip to spread a thin layer under the seam. Press lightly. Let it dry.

ship ahoy

An ideal design for a luxury yacht—or a little boy

1 Sail: Tear off 1 square. Fold in half diagonally.

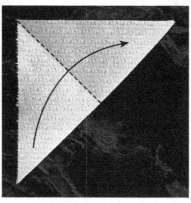

2 Fold lower tip up to the right tip.

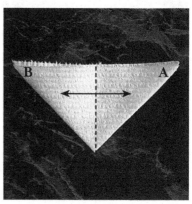

3 Fold and unfold Point A to Point B, top layer only, to make a crease.

4 Insert index finger into top right layer. Raise right half of triangle to vertical.

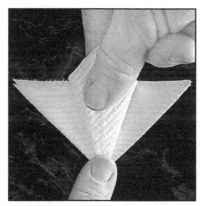

5 Position diamond shape at center of triangle. Flatten into place.

6 Set the sail aside.

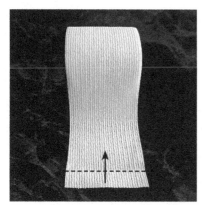

7 Unwind several squares from the roll. Fold the end up 1 inch.

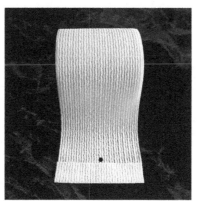

8 Place sail on roll with lower point of diamond at the dot.

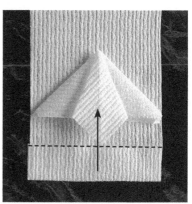

9 Fold end of roll up in a 1-inch fold.

69

10 Fold bottom corners under. Rewind toilet paper until boat rests against roll.

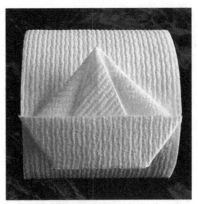

11 Finished.

Sailing, sailing, over the bounding main...

pleated leaf

Practice and carefully selected toilet paper are key to the success of this style. Choose a light, crisp paper that will hold a sharp crease. The pleated leaf is more difficult than most designs...but so magnificent.

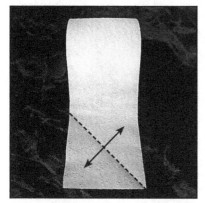

1 Fold and unfold left corner up to right side to make a crease.

2 Pleat the TP above and below the crease in narrow folds starting at "A" and continuing in the order shown above. Notice how the upper pleats taper to the left.

3 Stack the pleats. About 1 inch from the edge (see dot), twist the left side upward...

4 ...like this. Pinch the twist tightly.

5 Rewind the roll.

6 Press your thumb on the twist. Pull down on bottom pleat to shape the leaf. Adjust the folds for an attractive appearance.

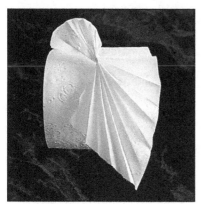

7 Finished.

Tip: The number of crease lines depicted in Step 2 is for reference only. There is no set number of pleats for this design. You will get pleasing results from various quantities of creases.

upsy daisy

Use this cute floral design for a vertical toilet paper holder or a spare roll.
Additional supply: scissors

1 Center piece: Tear 3 squares off of the roll. Crumple 2 squares into a ball; place ball on top of remaining square.

2 Wrap square around ball. Twist the ends together...

3 ...like this. Set center piece aside.

4 Petals: Tear off three 2-square strips from the roll. Stack them. Secure loose end of toilet paper roll with a diagonal tuck (see page 28).

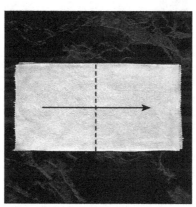

5 Fold the stack in half—on the perforations.

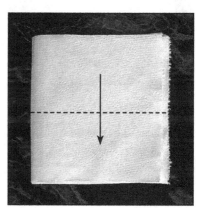

6 Fold the stack in half loosely. *Do not crease.*

7 Cut the corner of raw edges into a curve.

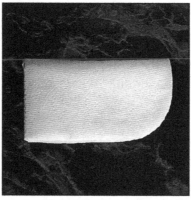

8 Unfold. Separate the 3 pieces from the stack.

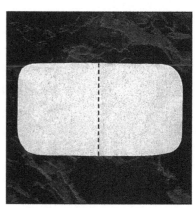

9 Pucker one piece across the dotted line until the end points meet.

75

10 Push the center into the core...

11 ...like this. Now repeat Steps 9-10 with the remaining 2 pieces—facing them in different directions.

12 Push the center piece into the middle...

13 ...like this.

14 Finished.

Tip: To add fragrance, place a few drops of essential oil inside the cardboard core. Try lavender, rose, jasmine or geranium for a lovely floral scent.

pumpkin

1 Face: Unwind a short length of paper from roll and fold the first square under.

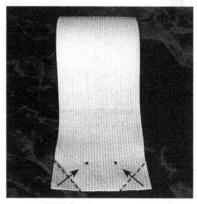

2 Fold corners up to dots, making the distance between front edge and dots about 1½ inches.

3 Fold edge up to the next row of perforations (a 2-inch fold).

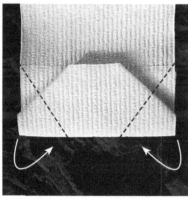

4 Fold corners under, adjusting folds to form a symmetric hexagon.

5 Optional: Use a sharp knife (adults only) to cut a new pencil eraser into a triangle shape. Use this to stamp a face on your pumpkin.

6 Stem: Tear off 1 square of TP and fold it in half diagonally.

7 Starting at Point X, roll triangle into a tube.

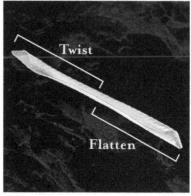

8 Twist half of the tube tightly. Flatten the other half.

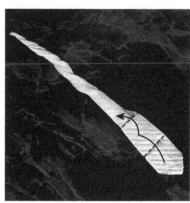

9 Make two 1-inch folds in the flattened half of the stem.

79

10 Insert the stem into the pumpkin. Rewind the roll until the pumpkin lays nicely across the front.

11 Finished.

Pumpkin Face Template

reindeer

Additional supplies: 2 small twigs; 2 new pencils; black and red ink pads

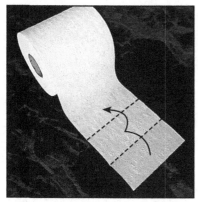

1 Fold the end up twice, making each fold 2 inches deep. (Most squares of TP measure 4 inches between perforations.)

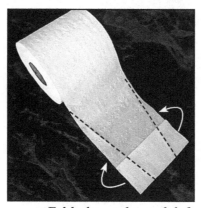

2 Fold the right and left corners under, adjusting the folds to make a centered and symmetric vessel.

3 Using a sharp knife (adults only), cut a new pencil eraser in half to stamp black eyes on your reindeer. Use an uncut pencil eraser to stamp a red nose.

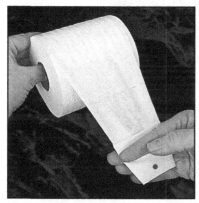

4 Rewind roll by grasping the end between your index and middle fingers while applying gentle tension with your other hand.

5 Put twigs in vessel for antlers.

6 Finished.

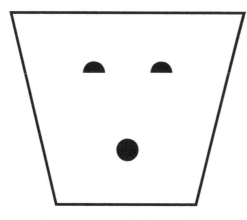

Reindeer Face Template

Tip: Quarter-inch round stickers can be used for the Reindeer face instead of stamping; use one for the nose and cut one in half for the eyes.

83

bow tie

Who knew bath tissue could look so dapper?

1 Tear off a 2-square strip of TP and set it aside.

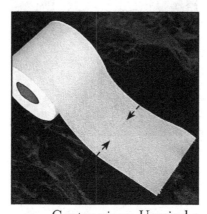

2 Center piece: Unwind a short length of TP from the roll. Tear each side on the first perforation leaving a 1-inch section intact at the center. See Step 3 for a tip.

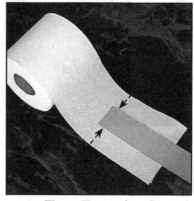

3 Tip: To make Step 2 easier, cut a 1 x 6-inch piece of cardboard. Place cardboard as shown. Press down on cardboard and tear up to each edge.

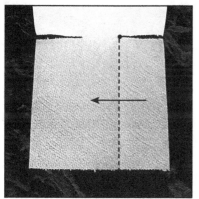

4 Fold right side inward at the dot.

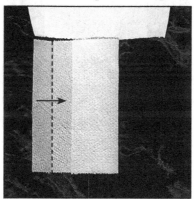

5 Fold left side inward so that raw edges meet.

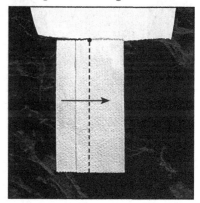

6 Fold left side inward at the dot.

7 Get the strip you set aside at Step 1.

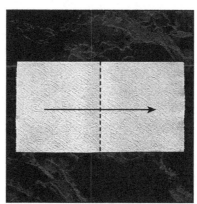

8 Fold in half on the perforation.

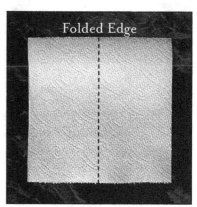

9 Pinch and pucker the paper across the dotted line until the end points meet.

10 Place bow on center piece, about 1 inch from lower edge.

11 Fold lower dot to the upper dot.

12 Fold lower dot to the upper dot, flipping the bow over as you fold.

13 Fold lower dot to the upper dot, flipping the bow over as you fold.

14 Press firmly on center to set bow in place. Fluff sides into shape. Rewind the roll.

15 Finished.

16 Option 2: Fanfold the paper at Step 9 for a different look.

shooting star

1 Insert: Tear off 1 square. Fold in half diagonally.

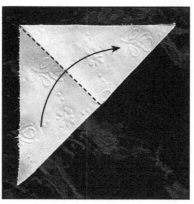

2 Fold the triangle in half.

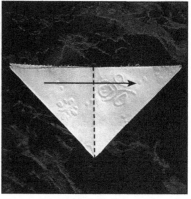

3 Now fold this triangle in half.

4 Set the Insert aside.

5 Tip: If the triangle has a ragged edge from TP that is not perfectly square, fold the ragged edge under—or cut it off—to get a nice, even triangle.

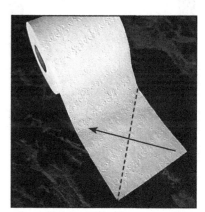

6 With TP flowing over the roll, fold the right corner up to the left side.

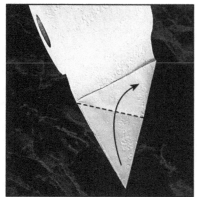

7 Fold the tip to the right corner.

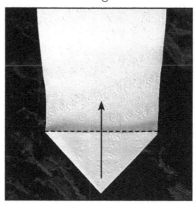

8 Fold the triangle up.

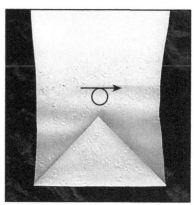

9 Flip roll horizontally.

89

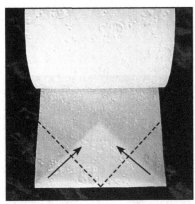

10 Fold the corners up to the center.

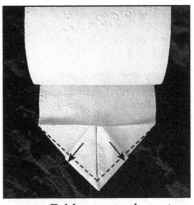

11 Fold corners down in a tapered narrow fold.

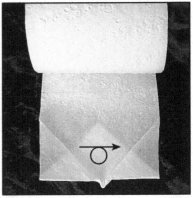

12 Rewind roll and flip it over.

13 Slide the Insert from Step 3 down into the diamond.

14 Finished.

90

fandango

This showy fold is fantastic for any format of toilet paper holder—vertical or horizontal.

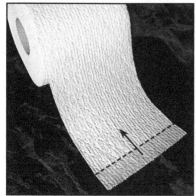

1 Fold the end up about ¾ inch.

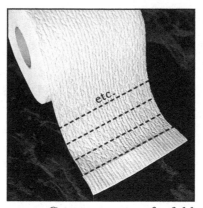

2 Continue to fanfold in ¾-inch pleats until you have made 20 more creases.

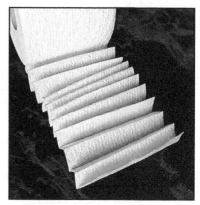

3 Stack the pleats.

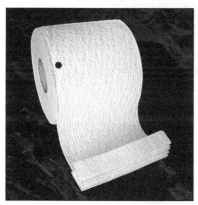

4 Press your thumb on left side of roll—about 4 inches above stack of pleats (see dot)—and grip right side of stack...

5 ...like this. Flip pleats clockwise and tuck end into core. Tip: With a horizontal TP holder, lift roll and wedge pleats between top of core and spindle.

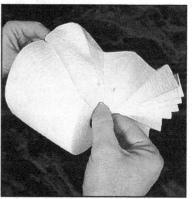

6 Adjust the folds for a pleasing appearance.

7 Finished.

Tip: To control your roll's position on a horizontal toilet paper holder, squeeze the roll to reshape the core until the roll balances where desired.

tropical fish

1 Fin: Tear off 1 square. Fold in half diagonally.

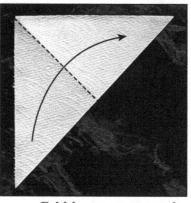

2 Fold lower tip up to the right tip.

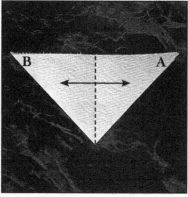

3 Fold and unfold Point A to Point B, top layer only, to make a crease.

4 Insert index finger into top right layer. Raise right half of triangle to vertical.

5 Position diamond shape at center of triangle. Flatten into place.

6 Set fin aside.

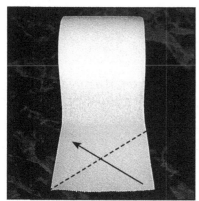

7 Body: Unwind several squares from the roll. Fold right corner up to left side.

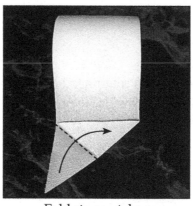

8 Fold tip to right corner.

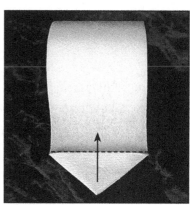

9 Fold triangle up.

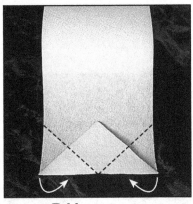

10 Fold corners to center back.

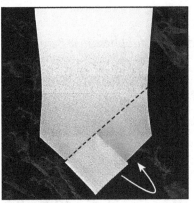

11 Fold diamond to the back.

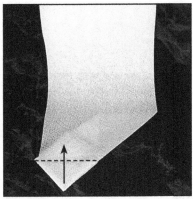

12 Fold diamond to the front: as you fold, the TP will automatically crease along right side of roll and at lower right edge of the diamond...

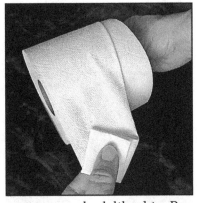

13 ...to look like this. Rewind roll by grasping the diamond securely with one hand while applying gentle tension with your other hand.

14 Insert fin into right side of diamond.

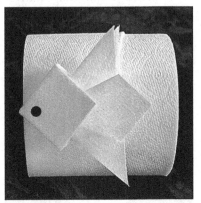

15 Eye: Using the eraser of a new pencil and an ink pad, stamp an eye on your fish. Finished.

Tips:
- *Apply a slight dab of hand lotion with your fingertip to secure the fish in position, if desired.*
- *A quarter-inch round sticker can be used for the eye instead of stamping.*

corsage

Use this for a vertical toilet paper holder—or as a lovely way to display a spare roll.
Additional supply: hand lotion

1 Leaves: Tear off a strip of 3 squares. Fold lower corners up to meet top sides.

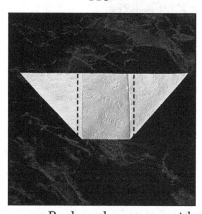

2 Pucker the paper with your fingertips along the dotted lines until the ends of each line meet…

3 …like this. Twist to secure.

4 Set leaves aside.

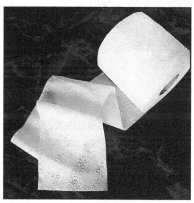

5 Flower: With TP flowing from under the roll, unwind 5 squares. Moisten your fingertips with hand lotion.

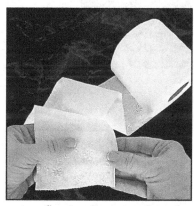

6 Start rolling one lengthwise edge of the strip. Roll tightly, just enough to hide the raw edge.

7 Continue until you have rolled along one side of 5 squares.

8 Flip roll and position strip so that the rolled edge is facing away from you. Start shaping the flower by puckering along the center of the strip…

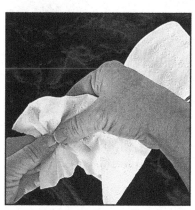

9 …like this. Gradually shorten the length of the strip and create fullness by working the paper in a push—pucker—push—pucker manner.

99

10 Work in a circular fashion — around and around — shaping the flower as you go.

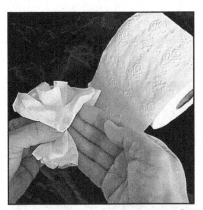

11 When you have puckered your way down the 5 squares, pinch and twist the lower half of the flower to compress the paper.

12 Put the leaves against the blossom to make a pretty corsage.

13 Unwind TP so that you have about 5 inches of excess beyond the base of the flower.

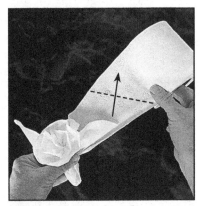

14 Press thumb against side of roll. Use your thumb as the pivot point and fold the tail end up...

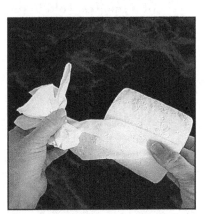

15 ...like this...

16 ...and insert corsage into the core.

17 Finished.

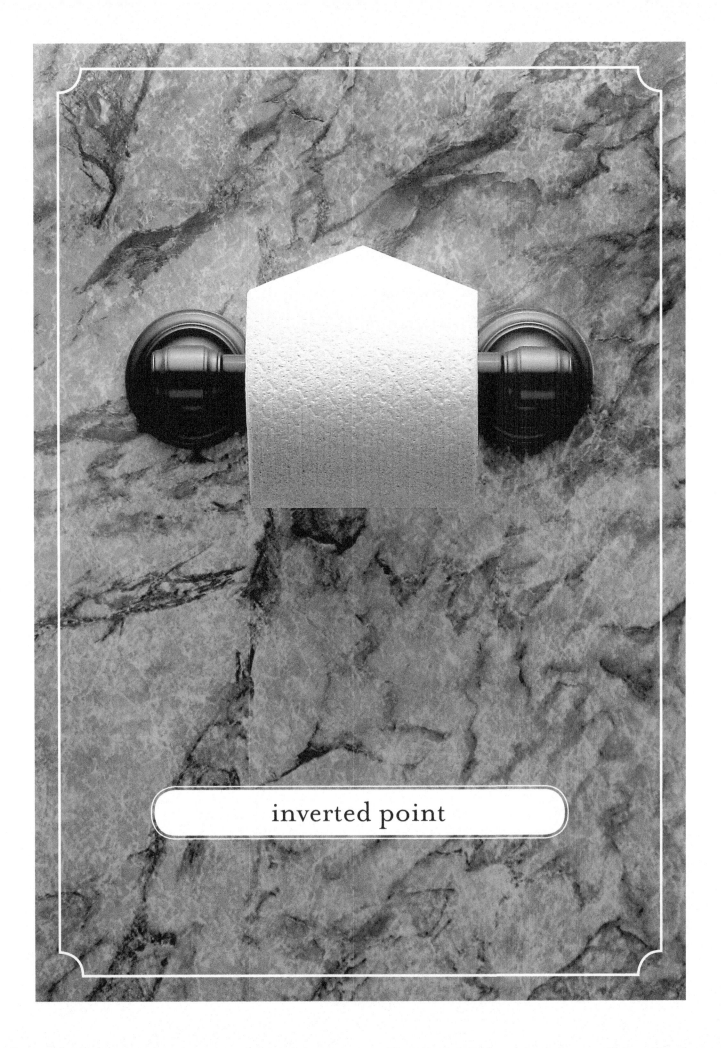

inverted point

This topsy-turvy version of a classic fold demonstrates that the tip can point up or down—depending on whether you prefer toilet paper hanging over or under the roll. The pointed fold is at its best when used in combination with rubber stamps, ribbons and embossing.

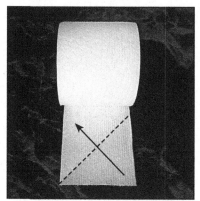

1 Fold right corner up to left edge.

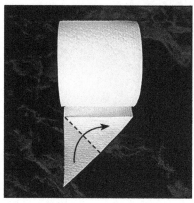

2 Fold tip to right corner.

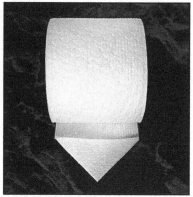

3 Rewind the roll.

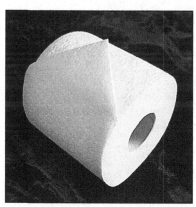

4 Finished.

Toilet paper used with a holder having a horizontal spindle has two possible orientations: the toilet paper may hang over (in front of) or under (behind) the roll. The choice is primarily a matter of personal preference. In surveys of U.S. consumers and of bath and kitchen specialists, 60–70% of respondents prefer "over". Many people hold strong opinions on the subject. American advice columnist Ann Landers said that the topic was the most controversial issue in her column's history. [*]

* Source: Toilet paper orientation, http://en.wikipedia.org/w/index.php?title=Toilet_paper_orientation&oldid=502443517 (last visited March 7, 2012).

rubber stamps, ribbons & embossing

Take simple folds from the previous pages—and dress them up with easy elements of surface design.

RUBBER STAMPS

Rubber stamping is an easy and effective way to enhance the look of your origami. Monograms, flourishes, corporate logos, and holiday motifs are ideal—or let your imagination lead the way. Ready-made rubber stamps are available in countless styles—including many that children would love. Custom rubber stamps can readily be ordered online; self-inking stamps are convenient. Metallic inks are especially elegant. Be sure to care for your rubber stamps by cleaning them with warm water and a paper towel after use.

RIBBONS

For a pretty pop of color, wrap ribbon around a spare toilet paper roll, thread a piece of ribbon through the core, or perch a bow on top. Choose colors to match your decor, or change them with the seasons. Sheer organza ribbon complements the delicate nature of bath tissue. Try printed ribbon for variety and interest. Wire-edged ribbon will hold its shape well when used for a bow topper. A stylish effect can be achieved by wrapping ribbon around the roll and securing it with a sticker.

EMBOSSING

Embossing can be done directly on bath tissue—or on a foil seal. A small hand-held embosser is ideal. The "TP" monogram above was made from Model 6001 at www.acornsales.com. For variety, additional seal inserts can be purchased for many embossers. Embossed monograms are classic; embossed logos can brand a business. Ready-made embossed seals of metallic foil can be purchased in many shapes and patterns; custom embossed seals can be made to order.

the end

Life is like a roll of toilet paper...
the closer you get to the end,
the faster it goes.

Additional copies:

Give a copy of

Toilet Paper Origami on a Roll

for a gift.

For purchase information, go to
www.tporigami.com

Learn more enchanting folds from the
world's first book of toilet paper origami!

· ·

Toilet Paper Origami
Delight your Guests with Fancy Folds and Simple Surface Embellishments
by Linda Wright

ISBN: 978-0980092318

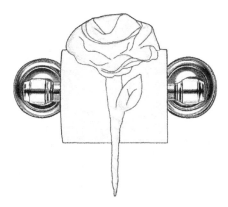

From hearts, flowers and fans to butterflies, boats and
bunnies, this collection includes 30 charming, elegant
and whimsical ways to style the end of a toilet paper roll.

· ·

For purchase information, go to
www.tporigami.com

Take toilet paper to a new dimension and
revolutionize your use of a bathroom basic!

....

Toilet Paper Crafts for Holidays and Special Occasions
60 Papercraft, Sewing, Origami and Kanzashi Projects
by Linda Wright

ISBN: 978-0980092325

Learn to make beautiful decorations, party favors,
cards, costumes, masks, garnishes, gifts and gift
toppers from a craft supply that is always at hand.

....

For purchase information, go to
www.tporigami.com

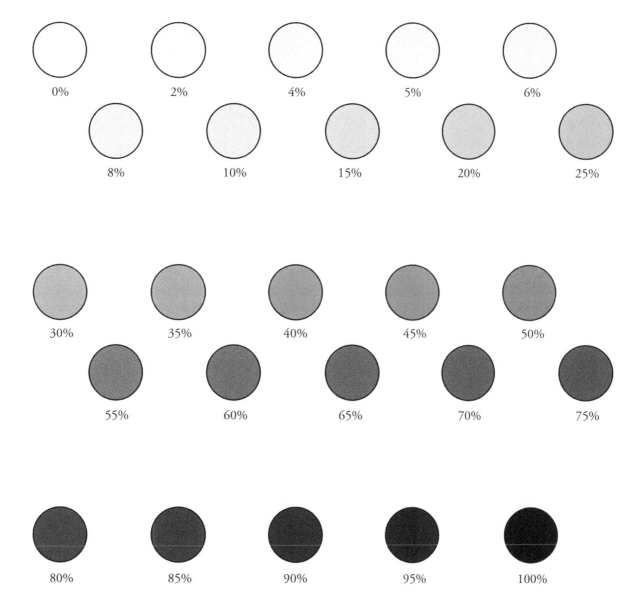

This dot gain chart has been inserted to help the publisher
monitor the printing quality of this book.

Made in the USA
Monee, IL
15 November 2020